The Fool

The Fool card is numbered zero, which is the number of unlimited potential. On this card, a young man stands walking joyfully on the edge of a cliff without a care in the world. As he embarks on a new journey, he gazes upward towards the sky (and universe) and is unaware that he is about to step off into the unknown. If he takes one more step, he is soon to encounter many possible dangers ahead. Is he naive or simply unaware?

Over his shoulder, he carries a knapsack containing all he needs (which isn't much). In his left hand, he holds a white rose representing his purity and innocence. The small white dog by his feet represents loyalty and protection, and reminds him to move forward with caution. As the dog barks at the Fool, he warns him to become more aware of his surroundings or he will never see all the adventures that he dreams to encounter. Behind the Fool, the mountain range suggests challenges ahead. Life's hurdles are forever present, but doesn't phase this young man. The Fool's only care in the present, is to start his journey ahead.

UPRIGHT: Beginnings, innocence, spontaneity, a free spirit
REVERSED: Holding back, recklessness, risk-taking

Astrology: Uranus

Element: Air

The Magician

The number one card, representing new beginnings and opportunities. The Magician stands pointing one arm up towards the universe and the other stretched down to the earth. This stance represents the connection between spiritual realms and the material. Manipulating these relationships help the Magician manifest his goals in the physics world.

The Magician wears a white robe symbolizing purity and a red cloak representing knowledge and worldly experiences. In front of him on the table, are the four suits symbolized in Tarot: representing the four elements – a cup (water), wand (fire), sword (air), & pentacle (earth). Proving he has all the elements and tools needed to make his manifestations a reality and being a conduit helps him convert energy into matter.

An infinity symbol above his head and a snake biting its tail around his waist, suggests that he has access to unlimited potential and opportunities. Lastly, the flowers and foliage in the foreground represents blossoming fruition of his goals and aspirations.

UPRIGHT: Manifestation, resourcefulness, power, inspired action
REVERSED: Manipulation, poor planning, untapped talents

Astrology: Mercury

Element: Air

THE MAGICIAN

The High Priestess

Here is the High Priestess who sits in front of a thin veil, decorated in pomegranates. The veil serves to keep casual onlookers out (only the initiated may enter) and represents the separation of conscious and subconscious realms (the seen and the unseen). The pomegranates are a symbol of abundance, fertility, and the divine feminine.

The two pillars, marks the entrance to her mystical temple. One is black with the letter B (Boaz: in his strength) and the other is white with the letter J (Jachin: he will establish). Duality is symbolized by these 2 colors (black & white)- masculine/feminine, darkness/light; Which are all required to enter this sacred space. She wears a blue robe with a cross on her chest, and a crown; Both a symbol of her divine knowledge and her status as a ruler. A scroll with the letters TORA (signifying the Greater Law), rests in her lap. The scroll is partially covered, reflecting that the sacred knowledge is both explicit and implicit–only to be revealed if the student is ready to look beyond the material world. A crescent moon at her feet, represents her connection with the divine feminine, intuition, subconscious mind, and the natural cycles of the moon.

UPRIGHT: Intuition, sacred knowledge, divine feminine, the subconscious mind
REVERSED: Secrets, disconnected from intuition, withdrawal and silence

Astrology: Moon

Element: Water

THE HIGH PRIESTESS

The Empress

This card depicts a beautiful, full figured woman with blonde hair and a peaceful aura. She wears a crown with 12 stars, showing he connections to the mystical realm and the cycles of the natural world (twelve planets and the twelve months of the year). Wearing a robe with patterned pomegranates, she sits on a luxurious array of flowing red velvet cushions. One cushion in particular, features the symbol of Venus; the planet of love, fertility, creativity, beauty and grace – which is the essence of the Empress.

The Empress is connected with Mother Earth and life itself, with beautiful lush forests and winding streams surrounding her presence. Her sense of peace is drawn from the trees and water, and is recharged by the energy of nature. Abundance from a recent harvest is reflected by the golden wheat sprouting from the soil.

In Tarot, this card is the perfect symbol of motherhood, Isis, femininity and fertility. The Empress is a creator of life, of art, business, and romance.

UPRIGHT: Femininity, beauty, nature, nurturing, abundance
REVERSED: Creative block, dependence on others

Astrology: Venus

Element: Earth

III

THE EMPRESS.

The Emperor

Within the Tarot deck, the Empress is the mother archetype and the Emperor is the father. He sits proud on his large stone throne decorated with 4 ram heads (showcasing his connection with the planet Mars and Aires). The Egyptian symbol of life is reflected by the ankh he holds in his right hand and the world in which he rules, is shown by the orb he holds in his left.

The Emperor wears a suit of armor suggesting his protection from any threat (even emotional and vulnerable responses). His passion, power, and energy for all life is mirrored by the ruby red robe he wears. The Emperor's wisdom and experience is reflected by his long white beard; and he wears a golden crown demanding authority.

An indestructible mountain range sits behind his thrown, signifying his solid foundation. Underneath, a small river flows suggesting that even knowing he has a hard exterior, he is also an emotional soul.

This card is a symbol of accomplishment, confidence, wealth, leadership, and stability. More importantly, it represents father, brother, husband.

UPRIGHT: Authority, establishment, structure, a father figure
REVERSED: Domination, excessive control, lack of discipline, inflexibility

Astrology: Aries

Element: Fire

IV

THE EMPEROR.

The Hierophant

A masculine counterpart to the High Priestess is the Hierophant
(aka the pope or teacher). He is a religious figure who sits between
two pillars of a sacred temple. The purpose of the Hierophant,
is to bring the spiritual down to earth. Ideally, to create harmony
in the face of crisis. When in crisis, the Hierophant can diffuse the
panic and offer practical input.

Wearing three robes (blue, red & white) and a three tiered
crown – they both represent the three worlds in which he rules
(conscious, subconscious, and super–conscious). In his left hand,
he holds a Papal Cross which is a symbol of his religious status.
A religious blessing is represented in his right hand; with
two fingers pointing up to the heavens and two down to earth.
Crossed keys lay at his feet, which represents the balance between
the conscious and subconscious minds. Not to mention, the
unlocking of mysteries (which only he can teach).

Two followers kneel before him, waiting for the Hierophants
wisdom and to be initiated into the church for their appointed roles.

UPRIGHT: Spiritual wisdom, religious beliefs, conformity, tradition,
institutions
REVERSED: Personal beliefs, freedom, challenging the status quo

Astrology: Taurus

Element: Earth

THE·HIEROPHANT

The Lovers

A man and woman stand naked in the beautifully fertile Garden of Eden. The Lovers are observed by the angel Raphael, who represents both the physical and emotional healings of life. While blessing the pair, the angel also reminds them of their union with the Divine.

Behind the woman, stands the forbidden apple tree with a serpent winding up the trunk – this represents the sensual pleasures that can take ones focus away from the Divine. Behind the man is a tree of flames, representing passion – the primary concerns for man.

12 Flames for the 12 zodiac signs, also symbolizing time and eternity. The man stares at the woman, who regards the angel – showing the path from physical desire to emotional needs to spiritual concerns (or the conscious to the subconscious to the super-conscious). Lastly, the (phallic) volcano in the background represents the eruption of passion between the two lovers in their vulnerable state.

UPRIGHT: Love, harmony, relationships, values alignment, choices
REVERSED: Self-love, disharmony, imbalance, misalignment of values

Astrology: Gemini

Element: Air

THE LOVERS.

The Temperance

This card can be difficult to interpret at times, but in general it's about the blending of opposites and the achieving of synthesis. While also reflecting peace, harmony, and patience.

This image portrays a large winged angel standing tall, representing both masculine and feminine (or genderless). On the front of its light blue robe is a triangle enclosed in a square – representing that the humans (triangle) are bounded by the natural law of the earth (square). Standing with one foot on the rocks and the other in the water, the angel expresses the need to stay grounded while also being in the flow. Additionally, the flow and alchemy of life is represented by the angel pouring water between two cups.

In the background, a winding path up to the mountains reflects our journey through life. A golden crown glowing above the mountains is a symbol of taking the higher path and the importance of staying true to ones true life purpose.

UPRIGHT: Balance, moderation, patience, purpose
REVERSED: Imbalance, excess, self-healing, re-alignment

Astrology: Sagittarius

Element: Fire

XIV

TEMPERANCE.

Strength

On this card, a woman is seen gently stroking a lion on its forehead and jaw. Even knowing the lion is known for its ferociousness, the woman has tamed the wild beast with her loving and calming energy. The lion is a symbol of raw desires and passion – by taming him, the woman shows that when inner strength and resilience is applied, animal instinct and raw passion can be expressed in a positive way. The woman never uses force, instead she channels her inner strength to subdue the wild beast.

The woman's white robe represents her purity of spirit – her belt and crown made of flowers shows her connection to nature. An infinity symbol hovering above the woman's head symbolizing her infinite potential and wisdom.

The Strength card in Tarot is all about energy and courage. It is a card representing bravery and fierceness (much like the lions hot roaring energy).

UPRIGHT: Strength, courage, persuasion, influence, compassion
REVERSED: Inner strength, self-doubt, low energy, raw emotion

Astrology: Leo

Element: Fire

The Tower

This card paints a scene of chaos and destruction. It also portrays the downfall of old ideas. Perched at the top of a rocky mountain range is a tall solid Tower. Even though the tower's structure is solid, it was built on shaky foundations; making the tower easy to bring down by a single bolt of lightning – representing ambitions and goals made on false premises. The lightning is reflected by a sudden surge of energy that leads to a breakthrough or revelation. Lightning strikes the top of the tower knocking off the crown, symbolizing how energy flows down from the universe through the crown chakra.

Two people leap head first from the windows as lightning strikes the building alight. The people are desperate to escape the burning structure, not knowing what awaits them as they fall. Surrounding the individuals are 22 flames, representing the 12 signs of the zodiac and 10 points of the Tree of Life – which suggests that even in times of chaos, there is always divine intervention. Even in destructions, there is room for something new to be built.

UPRIGHT: Sudden change, upheaval, chaos, revelation, awakening
REVERSED: Personal transformation, fear of change, averting disaster

Astrology: Mars

Element: Fire

THE TOWER.

Wheel of Fortune

The Wheel of Fortune card is one of the most highly symbolic cards in the Tarot deck. In the center lies a large wheel covered in perplexing symbols. Four creatures surround the wheel: angel, eagle, lion, and bull. Which are related to the 4 fixed signs in the Zodiac: Leo, Taurus, Aquarius, and Scorpio. Each creature holds a book representing the Torah, which communicated self-understanding and wisdom.

Surrounding the wheel is a snake, indicating the act of descending into the material world. Atop of the wheel sits a sphinx, and rising from the bottom is Anubis (or a devil). The pair are Egyptian figures representing both wisdom of the kings and gods (sphinx) and the underworld (Anubis). They rotate together, forever, in a cycle; suggesting that as one comes up, the other goes down.

This card is a symbol of destiny, progress, and unexpected events. Change is constant and inevitable in life, a never-ending cycle. The Wheel of Fortune is a reminder that good luck happens as quickly as bad.

UPRIGHT: Good luck, karma, life cycles, destiny, a turning point
REVERSED: Bad luck, resistance to change, breaking cycles

Astrology: Juniper

Element: Fire

WHEEL of FORTUNE.

The World

In a large laurel wreath, dances a naked woman wrapped in a purple cloth – looking back to her past, while her body moves forward to her future. Like the Magician, she holds two wands or batons. Which is a symbol that what the Magician has manifested has now come to completion in the world. The circular wreath is a symbol of a successful continuous cycle and new beginnings. Just as the woman steps through the wreath, she is completing a phase while beginning another.

Similar to those in the Wheel of Fortune card – around the wreath are four figures: a lion, bull, cherub, and eagle. The figures represent the four fixed signs of the Zodiac—Leo, Taurus, Aquarius, and Scorpio. The figures also symbolize the four elements, four compass point, four seasons, the four suits of Tarot, and the four corners of the universe; Bringing balance and harmony to your journey, these figures are here to guide you from one phase to the next.

This card represents the successful conclusion after all aspects have been accounted for. A journey has been completed, and a long-term project has finally come to an end.

UPRIGHT: Completion, integration, accomplishment, travel
REVERSED: Seeking personal closure, short-cuts, delays

Astrology: Saturn

Element: Earth

Queen of Wands

The Queen of Wands is shown sitting proudly upon her throne, which is decorated with two lions facing opposing directions (a symbol of fire and strength). In her left hand and all around her are sunflowers; symbolizing life, joy, fertility, and satisfaction. In her right hand she holds a wand with one small blossoming sprout signifying life.

Positively, the Queen of Wands can be associated with sustenance, warmth, and fidelity. Even knowing the Queen is bold and outgoing, a black cat sits by her feet -a hidden side which shows she is also in touch with the darker, lesser known side of herself (her shadow-self). The black cat is a reflection of her ability to grasp her deepest intuition.

The Queens of Wands stands for being attractive, energetic, cheerful, wholehearted, and self-assured.

UPRIGHT: Courage, confidence, independence, social butterfly, determination

REVERSED: Self-respect, self-confidence, introverted, re-establish sense of self

Zodiac: Aries, Sagittarius, Leo

Element: Fire

QUEEN of WANDS

King of Wands

Here sits the King of Wands, a mature male who is confident, strong, energetic, and optimistic about life. He is a natural born leader, fearless, motivated, funny, charming, and good with his words. However the King can be self-centered, hot-tempered, and controlling. But at his best, he is proud, passionate, loyal, honest, protective, and dependable.

Sitting upon his throne, he holds a blossoming wand which signifies life, passion, and creativity. His cape and throne are decorated with salamanders and lions – both representing fire and strength. Biting their own tails, the salamanders represent infinity and the never ending drive to move forward against all hurdles. The robe is a bright orange resembling a flame, with a crown shaped like a tongue of fire.

This card stands for being forceful, creative, inspired, bold, and charismatic. The King is never a passive observer. He believes in himself and has the courage of his convictions.

UPRIGHT: Natural-born leader, vision, entrepreneur, honor
REVERSED: Impulsiveness, haste, ruthless, high expectations

Zodiac: Aries, Sagittarius Leo

Element: Fire

KING of WANDS

The Moon

In the nights sky, a full moon sits between two larger towers. The Moon has always been an iconic symbol of dreams, intuition, and unconsciousness. Between the two towers, the path of higher consciousness is slightly illuminated by the dim moon light (unlike the suns light).

In the background is a small watery pool, which represents the subconscious mind. Crawling out of the pool is a small crayfish, signifying the beginning stages of the consciousness unwinding. Howling at the moon, a dog and wolf stand united in a grassy field; both represent the tame and wild aspects of the mind. One is civilized and the other is wild and feral; both depict our animalistic nature.

Everything in this card seems to echo the other, as if to suggest two possibilities. Each side of the path mirrors the other. As we journey down the path of life, we walk a fine line between conscious and unconscious; the tameness of the civilized dog and the wild forces of nature symbolized by the wolf. In the distance, the two opposing towers represent the forces of good and evil. The difficulties we face in distinguishing the two, can be depicted by the similarities between both towers.

UPRIGHT: Illusion, fear, anxiety, subconscious, intuition
REVERSED: Release of fear, repressed emotion, inner confusion

Astrology: Pisces

Element: Water

The Sun

This card radiates with fulfillment, optimism, and positive energy. It also represents the dawn which follows the darkest of nights. The Sun is the source of all life on our planet, and it signifies the life energy itself. Underneath the sun, the four suits of Tarot and the four elements are reflected by the four sunflowers growing tall above a brick wall.

In the foreground, a naked joyful child sits on a calm white horse. The child signifies the joy of being connected with your inner spirit and the happiness that occurs when you are aligned with your true inner self. The nakedness represents that there is absolutely nothing to hide; and has the purity and innocence of childhood. A white horse also signifies strength, nobility, and purity.

UPRIGHT: Positivity, fun, warmth, success, vitality
REVERSED: Inner child, feeling down, overly optimistic

Astrology: Sun

Element: Fire

The Devil

This card shows a creature that is half man, half goat (aka Baphomet or the Horned Goat of Mendes). Baphomet represents the balance between male and female, human and animal, and good and evil. With wings of a vampire bat (an animal that sucks the blood of its prey) a symbol of what happens when you give in to raw desires. With a hypnotic stare, he draws in those who come near him and entrances them into his spell.

A darker side of magic and occultism is depicted above him in an inverted pentagram. With his right hand he gives a Vulcan salute – Jewish Blessing; and in his left hand he holds a lit torch.

Naked and chained to the podium on which the Devil sits, stands a man and woman. Appearing to be held against their will, but look closer and see that the chains can easily be removed. The pair grow small horns and tails, a sign that they are becoming more and more like him (the longer they stay). While grapes and fire signify pleasure and lust.

UPRIGHT: Shadow self, attachment, addiction, restriction, sexuality
REVERSED: Releasing limiting beliefs, exploring dark thoughts, detachment

Astrology: Capricorn

Element: Earth

THE DEVIL.

The Hanged Man

Being suspended in time and a sacrifice of the greater good (and of martyrdom), the Hanged Man is the card of ultimate surrender.

Suspended from a T-shaped cross, a man hangs upside down; viewing the world from a completely different perspective. His facial expression is calm and serene, perhaps suggesting that he is hanging by choice. His halo around his head signifies new insight, awareness, and enlightenment. With his right foot bound to the tree, his left foot remains free. Forming an inverted triangle, his hands are bent and held behind his back.

He is wearing a blue vest for knowledge and red pants that represent the physical body and passion. This card is a symbol of trial or meditation, selflessness and sacrifice.

UPRIGHT: Pause, surrender, letting go, new perspectives
REVERSED: Delays, resistance, stalling, indecision

Astrology: Neptune

Element: Water

THE HANGED MAN.

Queen of Pentacles

A Queen sits on her throne surrounded by luscious floral gardens and blossoming trees, signifying her connection/abundance to Mother Earth and nature. Her throne is beautifully decorated with carvings of angels, fruit trees, goats, and all other symbols of sensual pleasure and material success. In her hands, she cradles a golden coin (representing wealthy accomplishments) with loving care and nurture.

A small rabbit pouncing near by, signifying fertility and how her life is alined and in the flow. However, the rabbit is a caution that we should all be careful where we leap when chasing successful endeavors.

This card represents a Queen who is nurturing, resourceful, bighearted, and trustworthy. The Queen is always practical and sensible, ensuring that her people are happy and secure. She is always ready to calm your fears and share the burden of all of your troubles.

UPRIGHT: Nurturing, practical, providing financially, a working parent.
REVERSED: Financial independence, self-care, work-home conflict.

Zodiac: Taurus, Virgo, Capricorn

Element: Earth

QUEEN ofPENTACLES

Page of Wands

A well-dressed young man stands in a barren land, boldly holding a staff with both hands. On top of the staff, he looks inquisitively at the green leaves sprouting; which signifies that he has the potential to find growth in the least likely places. He is a constant advocate, passionate about spreading spirituasocial advancements that lift up his fellow man. The young man is greatly enthused by his ideas, proud that he can make anything possible, even in limited situations.

In the background, the desolate land proves that he is living in a land that has not bared fruit yet. Therefore, his ideas are completely hypothetical. However, if he chooses to partake in the journey of his suit, his pure heart could lead him to better fortunes.

This young man wears a tunic patterned in salamanders, a mythical creature associated with fire and transformation from bad to good.

UPRIGHT: Inspiration, ideas, discovery, limitless potential, free spirit
REVERSED: Newly-formed ideas, redirecting energy, self-limiting beliefs, a spiritual path

Zodiac: Aries, Sagittarius, Leo

Element: Fire

PAGE of WANDS.

Ace of Pentacles

This card depicts a hand emerging from the sky, offering a large coin to whoever can take it. A new opportunity offering wealth, business, and manifestation in all its glory. Now it is on you, to take this gift and turn it into something sustainable and meaningful.

An abundance of lush foliage and white lilies are flowing in the background, with a small pathway leading to an archway. Beyond the archway of greens, soars mountain peaks along the horizon. This flourishing image suggests that the time is ample to push forward with our career and financial goals. A decision of these measures, will require hard work and determination (as scaling mountains is not easy). However, you should make the most of this opportunity while it's in the most abundant position.

In Tarot this cards stands for maternal force, practicality, trust, and prosperity. It reflects possibilities where security and abundance are concerned. When pulled in a reading, it is one of new beginnings.

UPRIGHT: A new financial or career opportunity, manifestation, abundance
REVERSED: Lost opportunity, lack of planning and foresight

Zodiac: Taurus, Virgo, Capricorn

Element: Earth

ACE OF PENTACLES

Ace of Wands

Wands are associated with fire and energy, the Ace of Wands is the core reflection of fire within the Tarot deck. This image depicts a hand emerging from the clouds, extending a sprouting wand as an offer of new opportunity and growth. Only some of the leaves on the wand have begun to sprout, which is meant to represent spiritual and material balance; as well as progress. The abundant landscape further confirms the possibility of rich growth potential.

A large castle sits in the distance, reflecting promising opportunities to become available in the future. With rolling peaks lining the horizon, we are reminded that there will always be hurdles along the way. However, they are easily manageable with enough effort.

This card represents creative forces, course, and enthusiasm. To pull this card in a reading, is one of constructiveness and confident energy working towards individual power and fulfillment.

UPRIGHT: Inspiration, new opportunities, growth, potential
REVERSED: An emerging idea, lack of direction, distractions, delays

Zodiac: Aries, Sagittarius, Leo

Element: Fire

ACE of WANDS.

Ace of Swords

A glimmering hand appears from a white cloud, a representation of the Divine. The hand holds an upright sword, a reflection of the mind and intellect. At the tip of the double-edge sword sits a golden crown draped in a wreath, signifying success, victory, and great achievement. His crown is used as a symbol of both royalty and the power to rule.

In the background is both mountain and sea. The pair can be symbolized as the limitless reach and distant lands that the swords can be used to conquer.

As the Ace of Swords is a reflection of triumph, the rigged mountains in the distance depicts a challenging road ahead. Whoever embarks on this journey, will need mental clarity to navigate this demanding path.

This card stands for truth, justice, mental force, new ideas, plans, victory, and fortitude.

UPRIGHT: Breakthroughs, new ideas, mental clarity, success
REVERSED: Inner clarity, re-thinking an idea, clouded judgement

Zodiac: Gemini, Libra, Aquarius

Element: Air

ACE of SWORDS.

QUEEN of WANDS.   THE SUN.   WHEEL of FORTUNE.   THE EMPRES

ACE of SWORDS   TEMPERANCE.   THE WORLD.   THE MAGICIAN.

THE TOWER.   ACE of PENTACLES   QUEEN of PENTACLES   THE HANGED MA

IV — THE EMPEROR.

PAGE of WANDS.

VI — THE LOVERS.

XVIII — THE MOON.

XV — THE DEVIL.

XXI — THE WORLD.

XII — THE HANGED MAN.

KING of WANDS.

XIX — THE SUN.

ACE of WANDS.

VIII — STRENGTH.

V — THE HIEROPHANT.

Made in the USA
Coppell, TX
11 February 2023

12587478R00031